Table of Contents

INTRODUCTION   Glossary for Introduction   1

SELECTION 1   Glossary for "The Screech Owl Who Liked Television"   1

Crossword Puzzle   3

Writing Practice   4

LESSONS 1–6   Glossary for Lessons   5

Fill in the Blank   6

Writing Practice   7

SELECTION 2   Glossary for "Unusual Creatures"   8

Word Search   9

Writing Practice   10

SELECTION 3   Glossary for "The Great Wall of China"   11

Jumble   12

Writing Practice   13

SELECTION 4   Glossary for "June's Tuesday Special"   14

Secret Code   15

Writing Practice   16

SELECTION 5	Glossary for "Down to the Bone"	17
	Anagrams	18
	Writing Practice	19
SELECTION 6	Glossary for "Sacagawea's Journey"	20
	Missing Words	21
	Writing Practice	22
SELECTION 7	Glossary for "The Farmer and the Beet"	23
	Make a Poem	24
	Writing Practice	26
SELECTION 8	Glossary for "A Good Book"	27
	Crossword Puzzle	28
	Writing Practice	29
SELECTION 9	Glossary for "Good Taste"	30
	The Matching Game	31
	Writing Practice	32
SELECTION 10	Glossary for "The Rock in the Road"	33
	Jumble	34
	Writing Practice	35

Level D Glossary and Workbook

Introduction

PAGE IV

enjoyable	giving pleasure
made-up	imaginary
multiple-choice	questions with several answers to choose from
tarantula	kind of spider
purse	bag carried by women
wild	living in nature; not tame
pets	animals taken home as friends

tarantula

"The Screech Owl Who Liked Television"

PAGE 1

screech owl	night bird with loud cry
editor	person who gets books ready to print
woodland	forest
driveway	path for cars from street to house
quivering	shaking, trembling
endeared (to)	became loved (by)
perch	place for bird to sit
burst	came suddenly
treated as such	dealt with that way
convinced	sure
cowboy	person who rides on a horse to take care of cattle

PAGE 2

firm	strong and sure
constantly	all the time
tempted	invited (to do wrong)
headboard	frame at the head of a bed
staring	looking steadily
screen	front surface of television
streaking	running fast

cowboy on a horse

Level D Glossary and Workbook: English 1

pouting	looking mad or annoyed
to his rescue	to save him from danger
scornful	treating with dislike
peering	looking closely
curled	bent
menu	list of foods
crickets	insects that make chirping sounds
gap	space, opening
cozy	warm and comfortable
tunnels	openings that make paths through something solid
utter	express; make sound
contentment	happiness
scientists	people who study nature
emotions	feelings
incident	happening, event
whisper	say softly
PAGE 3	
appearance	how something looks
behavior	how something acts
improves	makes better
beetles	small bugs with hard shells
PAGE 4	
closet	small room for clothes
drawer	sliding box in a dresser
lined	covered on the bottom
crash into	hit suddenly
unwillingly	with dislike; not gladly
cheerfully	happily
PAGE 5	
thrilled	very happy and excited
confused	mixed up; not able to understand
convinced	sure
neighbor	person who lives nearby

cricket

beetle

Crossword Puzzle

Directions: Using the clues given below, fill in the puzzle with the correct words from pages 1 and 2 of this workbook.

Across
3. a place with many trees
5. place where a bird sits
7. Sadness, happiness, and anger are all _____.
8. person who lives nearby
10. A _____ lists the prices of food at a restaurant.
11. place to park a car
13. dogs, cats, rabbits, parakeets, hamsters

Down
1. shaking
2. a place to hang your coat
3. how to tell a secret
4. small insect that hops and makes chirping noises
6. person who gets books ready to print
9. A lifeguard's job is to _____ people.
12. If you study every day, your grades will _____.

Level D Glossary and Workbook: English   3

"Unusual Creatures"

PAGE 16

unusual	rare, uncommon
creatures	animals
giraffes	long-necked animals of Africa
elephants	heavy African and Asian animals with trunks
monkeys	small animals with long tails
zebra	black-and-white striped animal of Africa
donkey	horselike animal; burro
relative	similar kind of creature
raccoon	animal with masklike markings on its face
streaks	long marks

PAGE 17

female	girl
male	boy
clicking	making short, sharp sounds
woofing	barking
bares	shows
logs	fallen tree trunks
caves	hollow openings inside the Earth
chomp	bite
extinct	no longer existing
species	kinds
official	recognized (by the state)
mammal	animal that has fur and drinks mother's milk
grubs	larvae, worms
float	stay near the top (of water)
startled	frightened

PAGE 18

cruel	causing others to suffer

PAGE 20

get itchy	feel the need to scratch

giraffe

elephant

Word Search

Directions: Find and circle these words in the block of letters below. They can be up, down, backward, or diagonal (on a slant).

caves	elephant	grubs	mammal	species
donkey	float	logs	raccoon	zebra

A	R	B	E	Z	E	G	Y
M	A	M	M	A	L	M	N
L	C	L	T	X	E	X	Q
D	C	F	S	S	P	R	F
W	O	G	Q	E	H	S	L
Z	O	N	P	I	A	B	O
L	N	M	K	C	N	U	A
D	R	H	C	E	T	R	T
N	V	F	O	P	Y	G	Q
C	A	V	E	S	R	N	X
U	Y	M	S	F	I	P	Z

Level D Glossary and Workbook: English

✍ Writing Practice

Writing Prompt: Describe a time when you saw an unusual creature. Write your description on the lines below.

> ☞ **Be sure to check your writing for**
> √ spelling
> √ grammar
> √ capitalization
> √ punctuation
> √ paragraph indents

"The Great Wall of China"

PAGE 21	
wonder	an amazing thing
emperor	ruler; king
designed	made the plan for
enemies	opponents; not friends
protect	keep safe
attacks	enemies using force against each other
constructions	something that was built
repaired	fixed
crumbling	breaking into pieces
harsh	rough, hard, severe
PAGE 22	
frames	shapes or forms
willow	type of tree
gravel	small stones
slabs	thick, wide pieces
brick	block made of baked clay
guards	people who protect
approaching	getting close
columns	vertical (upright) shapes
smoke signals	messages made with the clouds from a fire
attracts	makes people come
explore	investigate to learn
PAGE 23	
divided	broken up, separated
PAGE 24	
encourage	give hope to
PAGE 25	
assisted	helped
tourists	people who travel
ignore	pay no attention to

Great Wall of China

Level D Glossary and Workbook: English 11

Jumble

Directions: Unscramble the letters below to make words from "The Great Wall of China." Then write the circled letters on the line below to find the name of the mystery man.

1. SMRFAE   __ __ __ __ (__)
2. SRAHH   __ __ __ (__)
3. RBKCI   __ (__) __ __
4. YSTORHI (__) __ __ __ __ __ __
5. SUGARD   __ (__) __ __ __ __
6. ALVRGE   __ __ (__) __ __ __
7. NEEMESI __ (__) __ __ __ __ __
8. SGOTRN   __ __ __ __ __ (__)
9. RNWEDO   __ __ __ (__) __ __
10. WWILLO __ (__) __ __ __ __

BONUS

Write the circled letters to find the name of the mystery man:

_____

Who was he? What did he do?

_____

_____

_____

12 AIM Higher! Reading Comprehension: Level D

✍ Writing Practice

Writing Prompt: Why was the Great Wall of China built? How long did it take to build? Write your answers to the questions on the lines below.

☞ **Be sure to check your writing for**
- √ spelling
- √ grammar
- √ capitalization
- √ punctuation
- √ paragraph indents

"June's Tuesday Special"

PAGE 26

diner	restaurant
apron	cloth that covers one's clothes when cooking
stains	spots
steaming	very hot
balanced	held steady
forearms	lower part of arms
delivery	bringing and giving goods
grinned	smiled
order	what is asked for
clipboard	board with papers to write on
wiped	cleaned
counters	surface for preparing or serving food
jukebox	machine that plays music when coins are put in

clipboard

PAGE 27

pulled up to	drove up to
moustache	hair on a man's upper lip
gravy	meat sauce
splattered	splashed, spotted
giggles	little laughs
pinched	squeezed
cringed	drew back (from something nasty)
glared	stared angrily
scoffed	mocked; showed scorn
rolled	made a circular motion
lettuce	leafy, green salad food
pickles	cucumbers preserved in liquid
onions	bulbs with sharp smell and taste
congratulated	said she did a good job

PAGE 30

task	job
customers	people who buy something
messy	not neat

moustache

14 AIM Higher! Reading Comprehension: Level D

Secret Code

Directions: Use the Number-Letter Code to find the words to the question below.

Number-Letter Code

1 = A	8 = H	15 = O	22 = V
2 = B	9 = I	16 = P	23 = W
3 = C	10 = J	17 = Q	24 = X
4 = D	11 = K	18 = R	25 = Y
5 = E	12 = L	19 = S	26 = Z
6 = F	13 = M	20 = T	
7 = G	14 = N	21 = U	

__ __ __ __   __ __   __ __ __ __ ,__
23 8 1 20   9 19   10 21 14 5 19

__ __ __ __ __ __ __ __ ?
14 9 3 11 14 1 13 5

BONUS What is the answer to the question above?

_____

✍ Writing Practice

Writing Prompt: What were June's jobs at the diner? Write your answer to the question on the lines below.

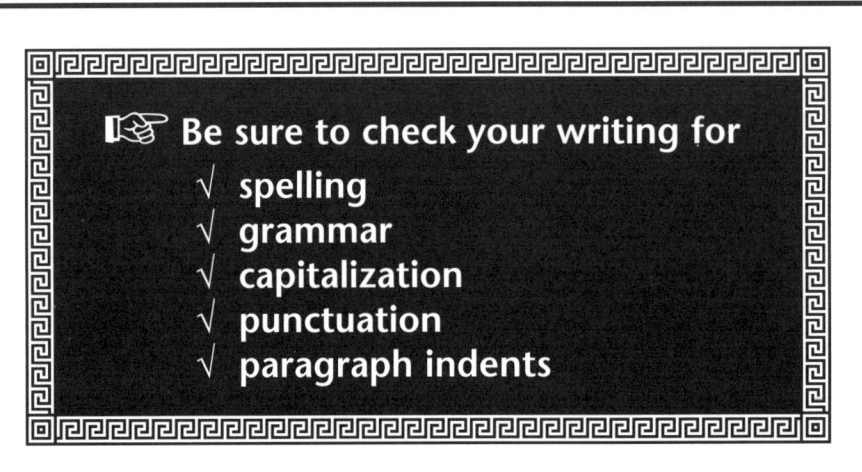

> **☞ Be sure to check your writing for**
> √ spelling
> √ grammar
> √ capitalization
> √ punctuation
> √ paragraph indents

"Down to the Bone"

PAGE 31

lost control	could not manage (the bike)
crashed into	ran into; hit
scraped	scratched
bruised	injured
swollen	grown bigger because of injury
emergency room	area in a hospital where people go for help after accidents
on average	like most people
slopes	hills
successfully	with good results
separated	not together
sponge	material that gets larger as it absorbs water
heal	get strong again

PAGE 32

straightening	unbending
wrapped	put around and around
snugly	tightly
crooked	bent
recovered	got better
screws, rods, pins	metal instruments
treat	take care of
needle	thin, sharp metal tube
prevent	keep from happening
calcium	mineral that strengthens bones

PAGE 33

cough; sneeze	make quick, loud noises caused by having a cold

PAGE 34

thinner	not as thick

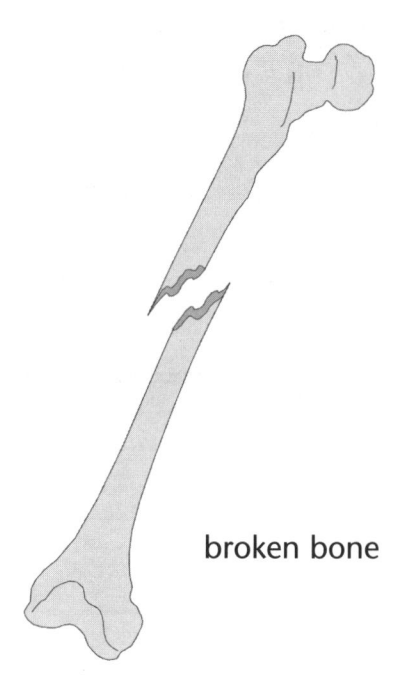

broken bone

cast

Level D Glossary and Workbook: English   17

Anagrams

Directions: Anagrams are words or phrases made by rearranging the letters of other words. See if you can rearrange the letters of each group of words below to make one of the vocabulary words in the box. (There are some extra words in the box.)

bruised	pins	separated	swollen
emergency room	recovered	straightening	treat
on average	scraped	successfully	wrapped

1. ride bus _____

2. draw pep _____

3. nips _____

4. deer cover _____

5. a dear pest _____

6. red caps _____

7. my one germ core _____ _____

8. thin rats in egg _____

9. well son _____

10. a raven ego _____ _____

Challenge: Try making some anagrams of your own!

18 AIM Higher! Reading Comprehension: Level D

✍ Writing Practice

Writing Prompt: What are some ways that a broken bone can heal? Write your answer to the question on the lines below.

☞ **Be sure to check your writing for**
- √ spelling
- √ grammar
- √ capitalization
- √ punctuation
- √ paragraph indents

"Sacagawea's Journey"

PAGE 36

purchase	something that was bought
deal	agreement
climate	weather
geography	form of the land
customs	habits
set out	started a trip
translator	one who changes words into another language
kidnapped	taken by force

PAGE 37

bounced	went up and down
supplies	things needed
chief	leader
settlers	people who come to live in a new country
pilot	guide
expedition	journey to explore
fever	sickness with high temperature
fond of	loving toward
adopted	took and raised as his child
territory	land
preserve	save
communicated	talked
earned	gained by work
continent	a major land area

PAGE 39

tours	sightseeing trips for visitors
treasure	riches
disappointed	sad

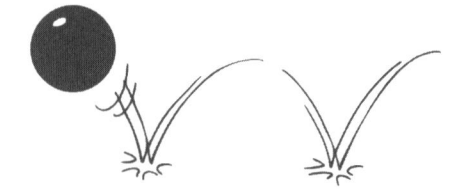

bouncing ball

treasure

Missing Words

Directions: Fill in the sentences below with vocabulary words from page 20 of this workbook.

1. When Rosa went shopping, she found a sweater she liked. She had enough money, so she decided to _____ it.

2. Before they went hiking in the Rocky Mountains, Andy and Matt studied maps to learn more about the _____ of the area.

3. When Veronica visited Mexico, she learned about the _____ for Mexican holidays like Cinco de Mayo.

4. Maggie got very sick one day. Her temperature was high; she had a _____.

5. Chris was reading about pirates. He wanted to look for buried _____.

6. Rick was not asked to the dance, even though he wanted to go. He was probably _____.

7. Ali took _____ of St. Louis and Detroit by bus so that she could learn more about the cities.

8. Emilio liked the warm, dry _____ in California.

9. Asia is a huge _____.

10. Before going camping for a week, Louis likes to make sure that he has all the _____ he will need.

Level D Glossary and Workbook: English 21

✍ Writing Practice

Writing Prompt: What do you know about Sacagawea's character from reading this article? Write your answer to the question on the lines below.

☞ **Be sure to check your writing for**
- √ spelling
- √ grammar
- √ capitalization
- √ punctuation
- √ paragraph indents

"The Farmer and the Beet"

PAGE 41

beet	dark red root vegetable
plot	area; piece of land
sigh	sound of sadness
hoed	dug
pantry	closet to store food
yummy	delicious, tasty
naught	nothing
pried	pull out forcefully
plucked	pulled out, picked
humongous	very large
stout	heavyset

PAGE 42

budge	move
tad	a bit
stubborn	refusing to move
stomp	hard kick on the ground
bleat	noise made by sheep
dislodge	move
nutritious	good for you
unbeatable	winning
beaming	smiling brightly
squeal	sharp cry
generous	willing to give
buffet	meal at which people line up to serve their own food

PAGE 45

joining	coming together to help
cleverness	skill, intelligence
endurance	ability to keep going

beet

Level D Glossary and Workbook: English 23

Make a Poem

Directions: Use the clues provided to fill in the blanks with the correct forms of words from page 23 of this workbook. In each pair of lines, the last words will rhyme with each other.

Jenny liked to grow good things to eat.

She grew carrots, potatoes, and even a _____.
                                              1. (dark red root vegetable)

Year after year, her garden did grow—

Larger and larger till it was too much to _____.
                                          2. (dig)

Her _____ was filled from ceiling to floor.
     3. (kitchen closet)

But year after year, she would plant even more.

One year she grew too much to eat,

So she fed the sheep who had just given a _____.
                                                4. (sound a sheep makes)

But so much food remained on the pile!

Jenny sat on a log and thought for a while.

Then _____ Jenny had a great thought.
       5. (kind)

She'd give her friends food that they would have bought.

So, she told all her pals to come later that day.

There was a _____ pile of food for them to take away.
            6. (very large)

When her friends saw the food, they couldn't believe it.

All were delighted for the chance to receive it.

They _____ food from the pile with smiling joy.
        7. (picked)

They loaded up the wagons for each girl and each boy.

When the pile had all been taken away,

Jenny went to bed. Then early the next day,

She awoke when she heard a noise in her house.

She ran down the stairs to look for a mouse.

But what she saw there made her start _____.
        8. (smiling happily)

It was a plateful of breakfast, hot and steaming!

Although she couldn't believe her eyes,

The breakfast was a _____ surprise.
        9. (delicious)

The wonderful meal hit the spot,

And Jenny was content on her own little _____.
        10. (area of land)

Level D Glossary and Workbook: English

✍ Writing Practice

Writing Prompt: What did the farmer learn from growing the beet? Write your answer to the question on the lines below.

☞ **Be sure to check your writing for**
- √ spelling
- √ grammar
- √ capitalization
- √ punctuation
- √ paragraph indents

"A Good Book"

PAGE 46

wallpaper	fancy paper for covering walls
construction paper	heavy, colored paper
pasted	glued, stuck
stapled	attached with a small fastener
illustrations	drawings
decorate	make pretty
diary	record of daily events
clouds	where rain comes from
castle	large building where kings live
picnic	meal eaten outdoors
recess	playtime at school
missed	felt sad about not having

PAGE 47

comfortable	at ease; free from worry
confident	sure
assigned	given as a task
opinion	what a person thinks about something
topics	subjects; ideas to write about

PAGE 48

erase	rub out, get rid of
recall	remember

PAGE 49

twine	heavy string
spiral notebook	books of blank paper held together by metal wire
yarn	wool string for sweaters, etc.
admire	think highly of
published	printed (many copies)

castle

clouds

Level D Glossary and Workbook: English

Crossword Puzzle

Directions: Using the clues given below, fill in the puzzle with the correct words from page 27 of this workbook.

Across
3. fancy paper for covering walls
5. playtime at school
7. remember
8. attached with a small fastener
9. ideas to write about
10. big stone building for kings and queens

Down
1. heavy string
2. drawings
4. think highly of
6. where rain comes from

✍ Writing Practice

Writing Prompt: If you had a chance to write every day, what would you write about? On the lines below, describe three topics that you would like to write about.

☞ Be sure to check your writing for
- √ spelling
- √ grammar
- √ capitalization
- √ punctuation
- √ paragraph indents

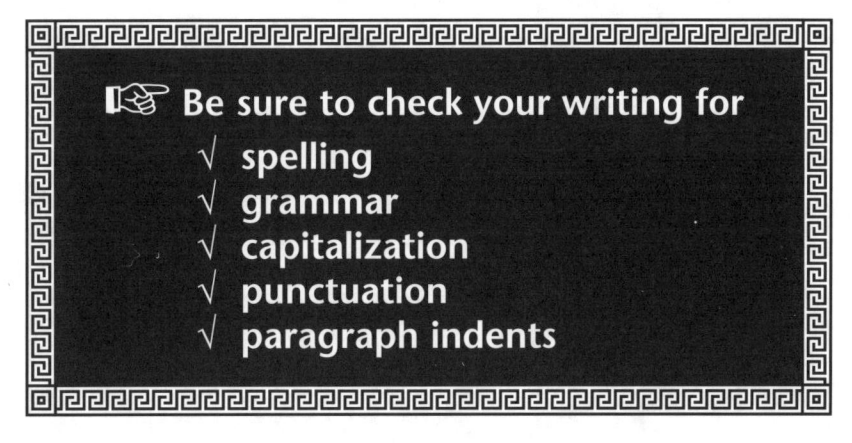

"Good Taste"	
PAGE 50	
wiggle	move back and forth
experiment	test
sweet	having a taste like sugar
bitter	having a sharp, unpleasant taste
sour	having a taste like lemons
cotton swab	little stick with cotton tip
PAGE 51	
chemicals	basic substances of which something is made
rotten	spoiled; bad to eat
avoids	stays away from
worms	animals that crawl underground
PAGE 52	
limited	lacking abilities
PAGE 53	
spicy	having a strong, hot flavor
PAGE 54	
crunchy	making a noisy, crackling sound
slimy	gooey, slippery
gobble	eat quickly

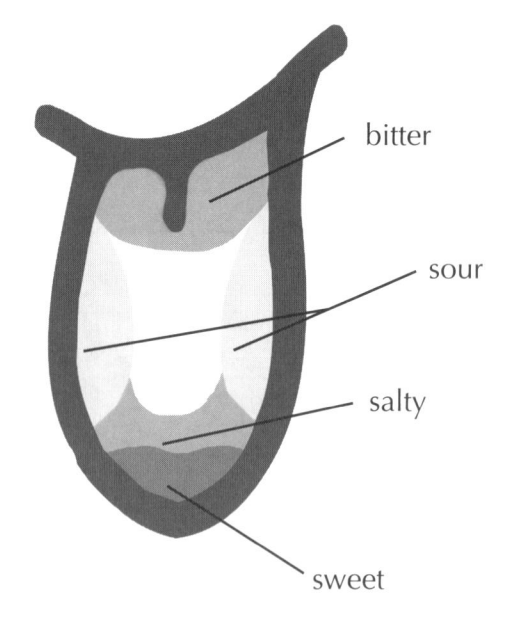

worms

The Matching Game

Directions: Draw a line between each pair of OPPOSITE words.

1. sweet
2. stand still
3. chew slowly
4. bland
5. good
6. avoid

a. wiggle
b. spicy
c. gobble
d. rotten
e. draw near to
f. sour

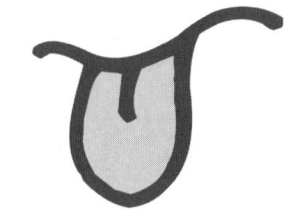

Directions: Draw a line from the organ on the left to the job it does on the right.

7. eye
8. nose
9. ear
10. tongue

g. tastes
h. hears
i. smells
j. sees

Directions: Draw a line from the food on the left to its taste on the right.

11. strawberry
12. lemon juice
13. potato chips
14. tonic

k. sour
l. sweet
m. bitter
n. salty

Level D Glossary and Workbook: English   31

✍ Writing Practice

Writing Prompt: What are three of your favorite things to taste? Describe them, using words you learned from the story about taste. Write your answer to the question on the lines below.

☞ Be sure to check your writing for
√ spelling
√ grammar
√ capitalization
√ punctuation
√ paragraph indents

"The Rock in the Road"

PAGE 55	
chatting	talking
shopkeepers	people who own stores
scenery	landscape; sights around her
sparkled	glowed, shone
citizens	inhabitants
PAGE 56	
grumble	complain
huff of disgust	expression of anger or annoyance
scowl	mad face
knights	men in Middle Ages with metal suits
trotting	riding a horse quickly
boasted	talked proudly
competition	contest, game
mill	building where grain is ground into flour
tugged	pulled
earned	gained by work
rewarded	given something in return
PAGE 57	
trickiness	dishonest cleverness
PAGE 58	
community	people living together
PAGE 59	
insulting	treating with disrespect

rock

knights

Level D Glossary and Workbook: English 33

Jumble

Directions: Unscramble the letters to make words from page 33 of this workbook.

1. YESERNC   _ _(_)_ _ _ _ _
2. TBDEOAS   _ _(_)_ _ _ _ _
3. PKESEHSOPER _ _ _(_)_ _ _ _ _ _ _
4. DENRAE   _(_)_ _ _ _ _
5. BLEMURG   _ _ _ _(_)_ _
6. GSHTKIN   _ _(_)_ _ _ _
7. GNITTHAC   _ _(_)_ _ _ _ _
8. GLUSINTIN   _ _ _ _ _ _ _(_)_
9. ZICTISNE   (_)_ _ _ _ _ _ _
10. KARLESPD   _ _(_)_ _ _ _ _

BONUS Read the circled letters down to find the name of the kingdom in the story.

_____

34   AIM Higher! Reading Comprehension: Level D

✍ Writing Practice

Writing Prompt: What was the point of putting the rock in the road? Write your answer to the question on the lines below.

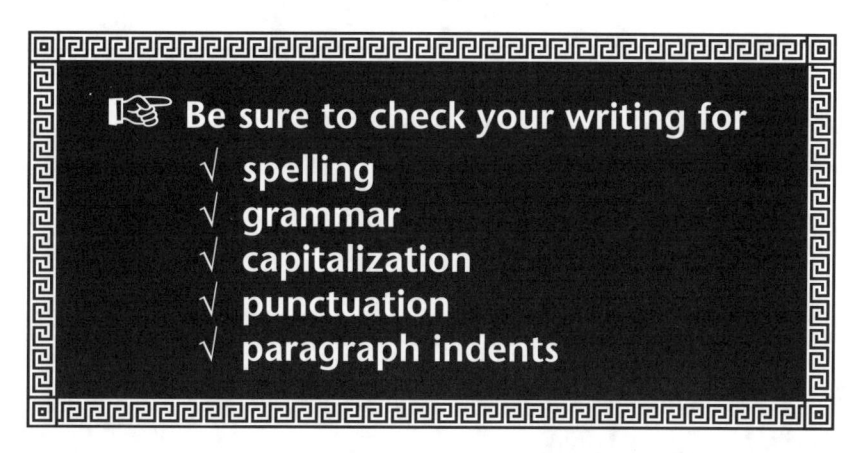

☞ **Be sure to check your writing for**
- √ spelling
- √ grammar
- √ capitalization
- √ punctuation
- √ paragraph indents

Notes

AIM HIGHER

English Study Guide and Workbook

SHEPHERD • CASTRO • SKEA • CHOI

LEVEL D

aim
advanced instructional materials

The Future of Education, Today

Beverly, Massachusetts
Farmingdale, New Jersey

STAFF CREDITS:

PUBLISHER
  Robert D. Shepherd

EDITORIAL STAFF
  Diane Perkins Castro
  Annie Sun Choi
  Kelsey Stevenson Skea

PRODUCTION & DESIGN STAFF
  Matthew Pasquerella

OTHER CONTRIBUTOR
  Michelle Castro

No part of this publication may be stored in an information retrieval system or reproduced in any form—by photocopying, scanning, reproduction in a database, posting on the Internet, or by any other means—without prior written permission from the publisher.

© 2001 Advanced Instructional Materials, Inc.
All rights reserved.

First Edition

Printed in the United States of America

05 04 03 02 01   10 9 8 7 6 5 4 3 2 1

ISBN: 1-58171-283-9

Advanced Instructional Materials, Inc.
100 Cummings Center, Suite 146Q
Beverly, MA 01915
Sales Office: 1-800-552-1377
Visit our Web site at http://www.higheraim.com